ANIMALS
at WORK

Camels and Llamas
at Work

Julia Barnes

GARETH**STEVENS**,INC.

A Member of the WRC Media Family of Companies

Please visit our Web site at: www.garethstevens.com
For a free color catalog describing Gareth Stevens Publishing's list of high-quality books
and multimedia programs, call 1-800-542-2595 (USA) or 1-800-387-3178 (Canada).
Gareth Stevens Publishing's fax: (414) 332-3567.

Library of Congress Cataloging-in-Publication Data

Barnes, Julia, 1955-
    Camels and llamas at work / Julia Barnes.— North American ed.
      p. cm. — (Animals at work)
    Includes bibliographical references and index.
    ISBN 0-8368-6222-8 (lib. bdg.)
    1. Camels—Juvenile literature. 2. Llamas—Juvenile literature. 3. Working
  animals—Juvenile literature. I. Title.
  SF401.C2B37 2006
  636.2'95—dc22
                                     2005054065

This North American edition first published in 2006 by
Gareth Stevens Publishing
A Member of the WRC Media Family of Companies
330 West Olive Street, Suite 100
Milwaukee, WI 53212 USA

This U.S. edition copyright © 2006 by Gareth Stevens, Inc. Original edition copyright © 2005 by Westline
Publishing. Original edition copyright © 2005 by Westline Publishing, The Warren, Aylburton, Lydney,
Gloucestershire, GL15 6DX.

Gareth Stevens editor: Carol Ryback
Gareth Stevens designer: Charlie Dahl

Photo Credits:
Brian Cassey Photography: 20. Roseland Llamas: 22, 23, 24, 26, 29. Laura and Fred Keller of Yellow
Wood Llamas, Inc.: 25, 28, 29. All other photos: Westline Publishing.

Printed in the United States of America

1 2 3 4 5 6 7 8 9 10 09 08 07 06

Contents

Introduction

A family's Bactrian camel provides transportion.

Find out about:
* camels that carry supplies across the desert
* the camels' "miracle milk," which has special healing powers
* racing camels that take part in fast and furious desert races
* llamas that guard livestock, protecting sheep and goats
* trekking llamas that are the perfect companions for hikers or tourists
* therapy llamas that visit hospitals and nursing homes

Thousands of years ago, humans on opposite sides of the world discovered that two similar-looking animals made ideal service animals.

Since ancient times, people have used camels and llamas for transportation and to carry heavy burdens. These animals worked easily in conditions that no other working animals could tolerate.

Camels (*pictured above*) are masters of the desert, moving effortlessly through the shifting sands, enduring extremes of heat and cold, and needing only small amounts of water. Llamas (*pictured below, right*) function well at high **altitudes** where food is scarce.

Although the world has changed dramatically since humans first tamed camels and llamas, these animals still play an important **traditional role** in everyday life.

The llama has worked with humans for thousands of years.

Where Do Camels and Llamas Live?

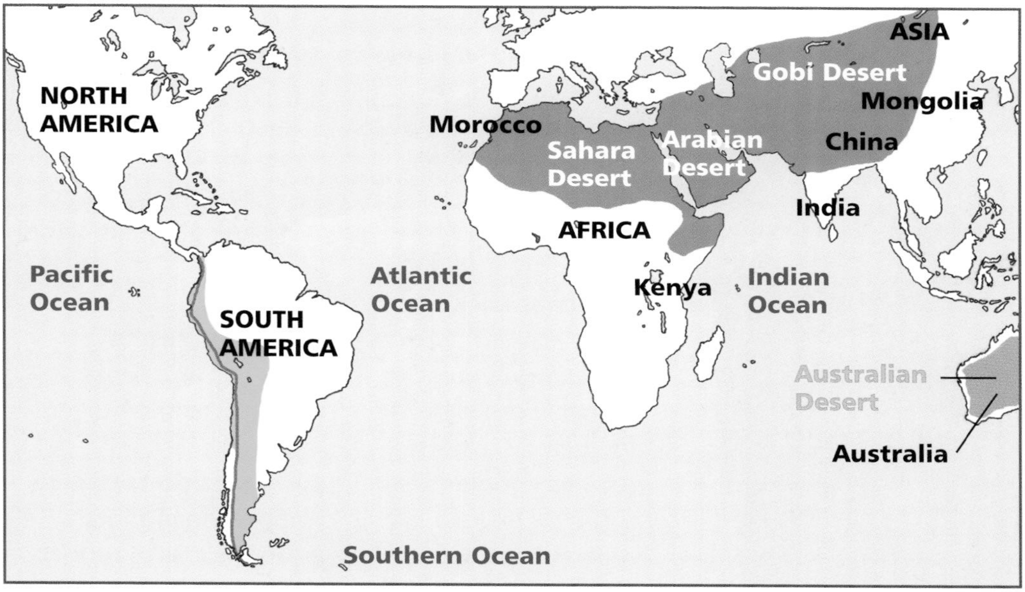
NORTH AMERICA
SOUTH AMERICA
Pacific Ocean
Atlantic Ocean
Southern Ocean
ASIA
Gobi Desert
Mongolia
China
India
Morocco
Sahara Desert
Arabian Desert
AFRICA
Kenya
Indian Ocean
Australian Desert
Australia

= native habitat of camels

= native habitat of llamas

= Andean Mountains

The map shows the areas where camels and llamas originated. Humans **domesticated** camels and llamas. Both types of animals now work all over the world.

Discovering Camels

Origins of the desert specialists

Camels and llamas share similar physical features. Both animals have small heads, curved necks, and long legs. Their split hooves help them walk over rocky or sandy ground. Camels and llamas would probably not win any beauty contests, but their bodies are perfectly built to live in extreme regions of the world.

Desert peoples of early civilizations quickly realized the value of these hardy animals, and they have worked alongside humans ever since. Today, more than one hundred countries — from Mongolia to Morocco — put camels to work.

Family roots

Camels and llamas belong to the Camelidae family. Their **ancestors** first appeared in North America forty to forty-five million years ago. The warm climate supplied these large, grass-eating **mammals** with plenty of food, so they thrived. About

The camel is specially *adapted* to survive in desert conditions.

DID YOU KNOW
If a camel or a llama is angry, it spits partly digested food at people or other animals that are nearby!

The camel can survive long periods without food or water.

two million years ago, the Camelidae family spread further around the world to South America and Asia, where they adapted to living in areas with little food or water.

Desert specialists

If you think of an animal of the desert, you think of a camel. The camel reigns supreme in one of Earth's toughest environments. It does well in conditions in which few other animals can survive.

A camel tolerates:

- severe water shortages. Deserts receive less than 10 inches (about 25 centimeters) of rainfall a year.
- extremes of temperature. In hot deserts, such as the Sahara Desert in North Africa, the temperature may climb to 122 degrees Fahrenheit (50 degrees Celsius) during the day. Temperatures can drop below freezing at night.

- bitterly cold winters. In cold deserts, such as the Gobi Desert in China and Mongolia, the temperature in January may fall to -58 °F (-50 °C).
- shortages of food. Camels sometimes go for long periods without finding any plants to eat.

DID YOU KNOW
The hottest temperature ever recorded, 136 °F (58 °C), occurred on September 13, 1922 in the desert at El Azizia, Libya.

The Art of Survival

Living in one of the world's harshest environments

Camels have developed some very special ways of adapting to desert life, which is why they are useful to us. Camels can travel in regions where humans can scarcely get a foothold, and they can survive on little food and water, so they are very easy to look after.

A camel survives in the desert because of the following physical adaptations:

The camel stores fat, which is a source of energy, in its humps. A Bactrian camel has two humps.

Thick fur protects the camel from the heat and the cold.

A camel's toes spread out so it can walk on desert sands.

A camel's nostrils can close to prevent sand from blowing in.

- It has a hump (or two humps) that stores fat. During long periods without food, its body burns the fat for energy.
- It has a very thick, split upper lip and eats desert grasses, thorny plants, and twigs that other animals do not touch.
- A camel can go for months without needing water. It loses moisture from its body very slowly. For example, a camel produces dry **feces** and little **urine**.
- Thick fur and underwool protect a camel against the cold. They also provide **insulation** from the heat and prevent the camel's body temperature from rising to the sweating point. (Camels are one of the few animals that can sweat.)
- The camel can also drink salty water, which other animals cannot tolerate.
- Skin connects the two toes on each of the camel's feet. The skin allows its feet to spread out and keep the camel from sinking in shifting desert sands.
- Hard, leathery pads protect the camel's knees so it can rest in hot sand.
- A camel can close its nostrils to keep sand from blowing in during desert storms.
- Double rows of long eyelashes protect its eyes during sandstorms.

> ### DID YOU KNOW
> Camels have proved so useful that camel trading is big business. At events such as the Pushkar Camel Fair in Rajasthan, India, hundreds of camels are bought and sold over the course of a long weekend.

9

One Hump or Two?

Recognizing the two types of camel

Two types of camels live in different parts of the world. The dromedary camel from North Africa and Southwest Asia lives in hot conditions all year. The Bactrian camel from Mongolia and China must cope with a bitterly cold climate much of the year.

What's in a hump?

Most animals store fat in their bodies, but only the camel stores its fat in a hump.

The fat in the hump provides energy for the camel if food is not available. If the camel is starving, its hump (or humps) will shrink, and may even hang down on one side. After the camel gets a few weeks' rest and

DID YOU KNOW

A simple way to remember the number of humps on each type of camel is to turn the letter B (for Bactrian) or D (for dromedary) on its side!

some food, the hump becomes firm and plump again.

The "Aussie" camel

Camels are not native to Australia — people brought them there.

The first camel (a dromedary) arrived in Australia in 1840. It was the only survivor from a group of camels that were shipped from Northwest Africa.

By the 1860s, hundreds of camels had been

brought to Australia. The animals were accustomed to the harsh desert conditions of Africa, so they adapted easily to the Australian Outback. Camels were often the only means of transportation for the early explorers.

In all, more than ten thousand camels were imported to Australia. Large **feral** herds many thousands strong now roam the Outback.

DID YOU KNOW

Today, there are many more dromedaries than Bactrian camels. Of the estimated fourteen million camels in the world, about 90 percent are dromedaries.

Dromedary (Arabian camel)

- **Humps:** one.
- **Coat:** short, longer on the head, neck, throat, and tip of tail.
- **Color:** white to medium brown.
- **Height at hump:** 6.2 to 7.5 feet (1.9 to 2.3 meters).
- **Weight:** 990 to 1,430 pounds (450 to 650 kilograms).

Bactrain camel

- **Humps:** two.
- **Coat:** short in the summer, with thin manes on the chin, shoulder, hind legs, and humps. The thick, dark winter coat reaches lengths of about 10 inches (25 cm) and is shed in springtime.
- **Color:** light to dark brown.
- **Height at hump:** 6.2 to 7.5 feet (1.9 to 2.3 m).
- **Weight:** 990 to 1,430 pounds (450 to 650 kg).

Desert Dwellers

The nomadic peoples who tamed camels

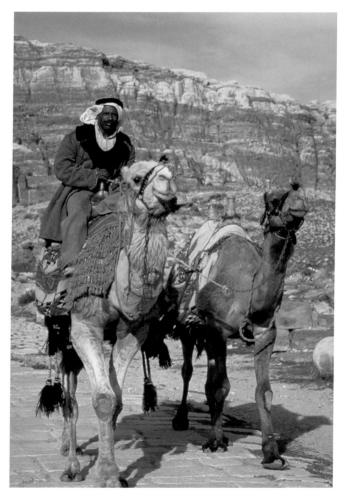

The Bedouin, like the other desert peoples, could not survive without camels.

Despite the harsh desert conditions, **nomadic** peoples have called the world's deserts home since the earliest civilizations appeared on Earth.

Nomadic peoples live in distinct regions. These include:

- the Mongols of the Gobi Desert;
- the Bedouin of the Arabian Desert;
- the Tuareg of the Sahara Desert.

Nomads have no fixed home. They live in tents and use camels to move from place to place as they travel across the desert and care for their herds of sheep and goats. People who are always on the move need

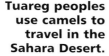

Tuareg peoples use camels to travel in the Sahara Desert.

reliable transportation, which camels can provide. Desert nomads cannot travel long distances on foot. The shifting desert sands, rough gravel, or rocky ground — as well as the scorching heat —make travel difficult.

Since as long ago as 250 B.C., the camel has proved essential to the lives and culture of the desert peoples. They could ride the camels. The camels carried food, water, and goods. Also, the animals could themselves be a source of nutritious food for the nomadic peoples.

Training camels

The Bactrian camels of Asia were the first to be used by nomadic peoples. About two hundred years later, the dromedary camels of the Sahara and Arabian deserts also became working animals. They were taken from the wild and were domesticated over a period of time.

Desert peoples were swift to understand the ways of camels. They trained the animals to accept being ridden and to carry heavy burdens. Eventually, the desert peoples began breeding their working camels to

produce young camels that were already accustomed to being around people and so were easier to train.

More and more camels became domesticated animals, fed and cared for by people, rather than living in wild herds out in the open.

Today, all the dromedary camels that live in Africa are domesticated. About two million domesticated Bactrian camels live in Asia, and about one thousand wild Bactrian camels roam throughout the Gobi Desert.

Ships of the Desert

Riding the sand dunes

The nomadic ways of life remained unchanged for many centuries. Even though modern technology makes desert life easier, the camel plays a vital role in the lives of the people who live in this highly challenging environment.

Riding camels

Nomadic peoples still ride camels. The animals are not as fast as motor vehicles — camels walk at a speed of about 3 miles (5 kilometers) per hour — but they do not break down, even when confronted with the worst desert storm conditions. Most working camels eat a diet of dates, grass, and grains (such as oats and wheat). If food is in short supply, a camel adapts to the situation by eating anything — bones, fish, meat, or leather — and more than one camel has been known to eat

Camels still provide the most reliable transportation in the desert.

A camel without a rider often carries heavy loads.

its owner's tent. The camel is called the "ship of the desert" because of its **gait**. Unlike a horse, the camel steps out using both legs on the same side of its body. This produces a swaying, rocking movement that can make a rider feel seasick.

Smaller camels are used as riding camels. They can travel up to 120 miles (193 km) a day carrying a rider.

Beasts of burden

Nomadic peoples must carry their possessions with them as they move from one place to another. The nomads must also carry enough food and water for the trek across the desert. Nomads use the bigger camels as pack animals.

An adult camel is a strong, tough animal that can bear heavy burdens over long distances. The nomads select the bigger, heavier camels for this type of work.

A camel can carry as much as 1,000 pounds (454 kg) if necessary, although the load is generally restricted to about 300 pounds (136 kg). Even with this amount of weight on its back, a camel can keep going for distances as far as 40 miles (64 km) a day.

The camel is so strong that it can lie down and get back to its feet with a full load on its back.

Camels naturally line up single file as they walk for any distance.

Camel Caravans

Opening up the desert for trade

A long line of camels carrying goods and people across the desert is called a camel caravan.

Gold of the desert
Certain areas in deserts contain rich salt deposits. Salt is an essential mineral for all living creatures, including humans. It has been an important trading item since the **Middle Ages**, when salt was first mined in the Sahara Desert.

Trade in salt — considered the gold of the desert — still plays a vital role in the desert economy. The method of getting salt from the mines to market has remained unchanged for centuries.

A camel caravan, with up to one hundred animals, is still a common site in Mali in West Africa. The camels

A camel caravan crossing the Sahara Desert.

Camel rides are popular in countries all over the world.

leave Timbuktu, Mali, and journey north, deep into the desert for 500 miles (800 km). The trek to the Taudenni salt mines, in the middle of the Sahara Desert, takes about fourteen days. The caravan loads up with salt and returns to Timbuktu.

Desert pathfinder

A desert specialist heads the camel caravan. He is an expert desert guide who has learned how to read the featureless desert landscape.

The guide must also specialize in weather forecasting and know where to find shelter if a storm erupts.

Boosting tourism

Although camels still carry people and goods in the desert, the use of four-wheel-drive vehicles — particularly if speed is a factor — is increasing. Camels, meanwhile, have found a new role in the tourist industry.

Worldwide tourism — including to desert regions, which were once considered too dangerous for the ordinary traveler — has become popular. In many countries, tourists sign up for camel rides in order to experience what it feels like to travel on a ship of the desert.

More adventuresome travelers take trekking vacations. These tourists join a caravan of camels and their handlers for a week or so. The camels carry the tourists and all the gear and food, and the tourists live like nomads. That way, the travelers can explore areas as remote as the Gobi Desert or the Australian Outback.

The Great Provider

How desert peoples use camel products

Camels are highly valued as a means of transportation, but for nomadic peoples the camel has several other important uses.

"Miracle" milk

Female camels (cows) produce milk for their young (calves). A camel calf must grow quickly in the unforgiving desert environment. Camel milk contains many **nutrients** for the **nourishment** of its young. The nomadic peoples also use camel milk as a readily available drink. At times, milk serves as a good substitute when solid food becomes scarce. People who get sick also drink lots of camel milk in the belief that it has special health-giving powers.

Today, a larger number of camels are being kept as "dairy" animals to produce milk and cheese. Camel dairies benefit countries such as Somalia in Africa, where it is too dry to keep regular cattle.

Fuel providers

During the cold desert nights, nomads light fires to keep warm and also to cook food. Finding wood to burn is difficult in a desert, but the nomads have a ready source of fuel — camel **dung**. Camel produce very dry feces

The camel not only carries heavy burdens, but also provides much-needed milk and meat.

Many countries use the camel as a work animal. The one pictured here helps haul a load in India.

(dung) — which is one of the ways a camel's body **conserves moisture**. Camel dung makes an ideal fuel for a fire.

Nothing wasted

In certain areas of the desert, water comes to the surface from underground springs or wells. Water may be available in such areas all year or it may dry up, depending on the season. These areas, known as **oases**, are extremely important to the desert peoples who need water to drink and to grow crops.

Some desert dwellers build permanent homes in an oasis and farm the land, while others stay at an oasis for the few months that water is available.

The camel is not always needed for transportation in and around an oasis, but camel herds are often kept at oases to provide meat and other essential, natural products. Camel hides make a fine leather, and the people weave the soft, woolly camel hair into material for warm clothing and blankets.

The long fur from Bactrian camels makes an especially good raw material for cloth.

Camels are becoming increasingly important in parts of the world where food is scarce. In Kenya in Africa, for example, camels increasingly provide a steady supply of meat and milk.

DID YOU KNOW
Scientists have studied the nutrients in camel milk to verify the claims that it can help fight infection. Researchers discovered that camel milk contains ten times more of the milk protein *lactoferrin* **— which has** *antiviral* **and** *antibacterial* **properties — than cows' milk.**

Racing Camels

Camel races are increasingly popular sporting events

The camel may not look much like an athlete, but it can reach a top speed of 40 miles (64 km) per hour. Camel racing has become increasingly popular in many areas.

An ancient sport?

Nomadic peoples started racing camels in ancient times when the animals were first domesticated. Recent interest in camel racing has spread throughout the **Middle East**.

The Bedouin peoples of the Middle East are huge camel racing fans, and camels that race are highly prized animals. Camel racing originated as a way to celebrate weddings or highlight festivals, but camel racing tracks are now big business in the United Arab Emirates and Saudi Arabia (*see page 5*). Races occur weekly, and the sport has a big following. Camel racing is also growing in popularity in Australia.

Born to race

As the popularity of camel racing spread, certain camels were bred specifically for racing. Now, camel

© Brian Cassey Photography

The fast and furious sport of camel racing is becoming increasingly popular in the Middle East and in Australia.

Smaller, lighter camels are bred especially for racing.

stud farms are devoted to producing racing camels. These animals tend to be smaller and lighter than all-purpose working camels. In the Middle East, two breeds — the Omani and the Sudania — have been developed purely as racing animals.

Camels start racing training when they are about six months old, and begin running races when they are about three years old. A male (bull) camel continues racing until he is about ten years old, but a female may keep going until she is twenty years old.

The jockeys

The jockey usually sits in front of the camel's hump, although the Bedouins traditionally ride behind the hump. Jockeys must stay on their camel without the aid of **stirrups**, and the only means of controlling the camel is by its head collar. It takes a great deal of skill — as well as an outstanding sense of balance — to ride a racing camel. Just like with horse-racing jockeys, the most successful camel jockeys are short and thin.

The races

Camels race 3 to 6 miles (5 to 9.6 km), depending on their age. Races last between ten and twenty minutes.

> *DID YOU KNOW*
> **A top-class racing camel is worth up to $250,000.**

Discovering Llamas

Origins of the mountain specialists

A mother llama is called a "mama." Her baby is called a "cria."

© Roseland Llamas

Temperatures high in the mountains drop swiftly at steeper and steeper altitudes. It also becomes harder to breathe. Mountaintop air seems "thinner" because it has less oxygen in it. The terrain also becomes increasingly rocky higher up. Few plants can grow in these conditions, and few animals can find enough to eat. The llama, however, lives high in the Andean Mountains of South America (*see pages 4–5*). Llamas are superbly adapted to the high life.

Tracing ancestors

Like the camel, the llama belongs to the Camelidae family (*see page 6*). The first camelids lived in North America, but the animal family split apart about three million years

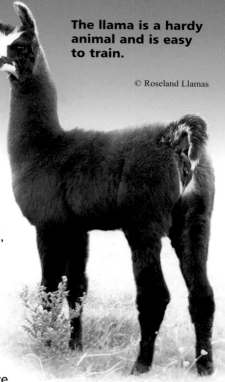

The llama is a hardy animal and is easy to train.

© Roseland Llamas

ago when llama-like animals moved down to South America (*see page 5*). By the end of the last Ice Age (10,000 to 12,000 years ago), no camelids were left in North America.

A new home

Four types of camelids live in South America:

- *Guanaco:* a slim animal with a long neck and a shaggy, reddish-brown coat. About 875,000 guanaco live in the wild.

- *Vicuna:* smaller and more graceful than the llama, only about 250,000 wild vicunas currently exist.

- *Alpaca:* descended from the guanaco, the alpaca is a domesticated animal, bred especially for its wool.

- *Llama:* also descended from the guanaco, the llama has lived with humans for about five thousand years — making it one of the oldest domesticated animals in the world.

Family skills

Several features of the llama and its South American relatives help the animals cope with the harsh mountain climate, including:

- A thick, woolly coat with a dense undercoat protects against the cold.
- Two-toed feet with leathery pads makes them sure-footed on the steep slopes and rocky **terrain**.
- A three-compartment stomach helps them survive on the poor-quality, low-protein food available.
- Unlike horses and mules, llamas do not suffer from the effects of **altitude sickness**, which causes extreme tiredness and lack of energy.

Beasts of Burden

The llama's traditional role

People who live in the harsh climate of the Andean Mountains must learn how to use their environment to their advantage. The Andean Indians saw wild guanacos and realized that the animals could be very useful to them.

The Indians caught some of the guanacos and soon began breeding herds of working animals that had never lived in the wild. Over time, the Indians found that alpacas produced the finest wool products.

The llama is useful as:

• *A Beast of burden:* The llama is the largest and strongest of the South American camelids. A llama can carry a load of 110 pounds (50 kg) for

© Rosela

Llamas can be trained to carry luggage on treks.

16 miles (26 km) a day, at altitudes of 16,000 feet (5,000 meters). The Indians used the llama to carry goods and food through the mountains.

- *A source of fiber:* Although llama wool is coarser and not as highly valued as alpaca wool, it is used for making clothing or for weaving into blankets. The Indians also turn llama fat into candles, braid the long llama hair into ropes, and use llama hides to make leather goods.

- *On the menu:* Ever since llamas were domesticated, their meat has been an important source of protein in the South American diet.

- *Keeping warm:* Llama pellets (feces) are dried and burned for fuel.

Troubled times

The Inca civilization, which developed in Peru, was one of the wealthiest in the world until its downfall at the hands of Spanish invaders in the early 1500s. The Spaniards brought in their own livestock (mostly sheep). They hunted guanacos and vicunas almost to the point of **extinction**, and llamas and alpaca became the animals of the poor, living only in high mountain areas where sheep could not survive.

Changing fortunes

The llama has only recently — in about the last thirty years — emerged from remote mountain herds to regain its place in South American life. Today, the llama is used in all its traditional roles, and is also boosting the tourist trade. Andes vacations that feature llama trekking are popular among tourists.

> ### DID YOU KNOW
> **About 300,000 llamas were used to carry supplies in and out of the silver mines when the Spaniards invaded South America.**

Living With Llamas

Understanding their behavior

Llamas are intelligent, docile (calm) animals who work work well with their human owners. Llamas are:

- even-tempered. If a llama is treated with respect, it will never become **aggressive**.
- quick to learn. A llama learns to perform many tasks.
- calm. The llama is a steady, patient animal that is not easily alarmed.
- sociable. Llamas need company. A llama may refuse to work if it is kept isolated.

Saying no

If a llama is unhappy with a situation, it makes its feelings known by displaying the following behaviors, including:

- spitting. A llama will spit partly digested food at a rival llama at mealtimes or in the breeding season. The llama may also spit at a person who handles it roughly.
- lying down. If a llama feels too weighted down, it simply lies down and refuses to get up until its burden has been lightened.

A llama often becomes an important member of the family.

© Roseland Llamas

Broadening Horizons

New jobs in new countries

The good reputation of the llama as a hardy animal that is easy to raise and keep has spread far from South America. The llama now fulfills a variety of roles all around the globe.

Trekking with llamas

Ecotourism, which lets tourists experience the many wild, remote places of the world, is gaining in popularity. Llamas provide a welcome service for hikers and campers in remote locations.

The llama can carry up to 30 percent of its body weight. Llamas often carrying hikers' supplies, and many tourists enjoy the added

Llamas are gentle enough for children to control.

Llama-pulled carriage rides are popular in the United States.

pleasure of hiking alongside these calm, peaceful animals.

Guardians of livestock

The llama plays a new role on large sheep ranches where coyotes or other **predators** are a constant threat. Llamas are always on the alert. If a llama senses a predator, it makes a sound similar to a frantic, quacking duck. The llama may even run toward the predator, kicking out at it violently. Llamas hve been known to injure or even kill dogs and coyotes that tried to attack sheep herds.

The wool trade

Traditionally, the bigger, stronger male llamas are used as pack animals. Females are kept on farms for breeding. They also provide a source of income for farmers through their wool, or **fleece**. Yarn and fabric goods made from llama fleece are popular items in markets around the world.

Driving

The versatile llama has also learned to wear a harness and pull a carriage or cart. It can respond to three basic commands: "walk," "jog," and "run." A leisurely ride in a llama-pulled carriage adds a unique twist to a sight-seeing jaunt or provides romantic transportation for a wedding party.

Performance llamas

Developing a high-quality llama herd takes time and careful breeding. Llama breeders are proud of the animals they raise, and a number of organizations dedicated to showing llamas uphold the breeding standards. Judges assess the llamas physical appearance or the quality of their wool. Llama performance classes include novelty events that range from

Llama breeders show off their animals at shows.

egg-and-spoon races (the person leading the llama balances an egg on a spoon), to pulling a cart around an obstacle course.

Therapy llamas

Some llamas are trained to help people with disabilities. Although it might seem hard to imagine llamas in hospital wards or nursing homes, they have proved to be ideal therapy animals for the following reasons:

- Llamas are calm and easy to manage.
- They are naturally gentle and do not frighten children or threaten frail and elderly people.
- Llamas can be housebroken.
- They are inquisitive creatures that enjoy going into new environments.

Llamas have proved especially valuable when visiting children with special needs. Children with physical disabilities can be encouraged to reach out and stroke the llama, or even take it on a short walk. The visit is such a special event that children who have difficulty speaking often ask questions. For others, watching a llama is a simple delight — after all, how often do most people get to see a rugged mountain animal up close?

Five thousand years after llamas and humans first worked together, the relationship between them continues to provide new interactions that benefit both human and animals.

A mama llama with her cria. Females are kept on farms to produce young and provide a source of wool.

The llama's calm, friendly nature makes it an ideal therapy animal.

Glossary

adapted: adjusted to new conditions.

aggressive: ready to fight in an instant.

altitude: the height above sea level.

altitude sickness: illnesses caused by the lack of oxygen in the air at high altitudes.

ancestors: family members that lived in previous times.

antibacterial: a biological agent that has the ability to kill a bacterium.

antiviral: a biological agent that has the ability to kill a virus.

conserves moisture: uses water sparingly.

domesticated: an animal that is accustomed to being cared for by people and that often can no longer live in the wild.

dung (or **feces**): solid body-waste products.

extinction: the process of eliminating an animal or plant species from Earth.

feces (or **dung**): solid body-waste products.

feral: naturally wild or previously domesticated animals that now live in the wild.

fleece: the wool of an animal.

gait: the way an animal walks.

insulation: a covering that provides protection from heat or cold.

lactoferrin: an essential milk protein.

mammals: warm-blooded animals that feed their young with milk.

Middle Ages: the years from about A.D. 1100 to 1400.

nomadic: a lifestyle of never settling permanently in one area.

nourishment: food.

nutrients: the valuable substances in food.

oases: desert areas located above an underground water source.

predators: hunters.

stirrups: metal rings that support a rider's feet.

stud farm: farms that specialize in breeding and raising animals.

terrain: the type of landscape.

traditional roles: jobs that animals were originally bred to do.

urine: liquid body-waste products.

Find Out More . . .

More books to read

Camels. *All About Wild Animals* (series). Gareth Stevens (2004).

Harman, Amanda. *Llamas.* *Nature's Children* (series). Grolier (2004).

Jango-Cohen, Judith. *Camels.* Benchmark Books (2005).

Murray, Julia. *Llamas.* *Animal Kingdom* (series). Buddy Books (2002).

Ripple, William John. *Camels.* Pebble Books (2005).

Web sites

www.kidskonnect.com/Camel/CamelsHome.html
Connect to a variety of interesting Web sites on camels.

www.historyforkids.org/learn/economy/camels.htm
Learn about the history of camels.

www.sandiegozoo.org/animalbytes/t-camel.html
Get great information for your report on camels.

www.llama.org/
Follow the links to llama history, personality, and farms that allow visitors.

www.llamapaedia.com/
Find out what veterinarians have to say about llamas.

www.worldalmanacforkids.com/explore/animals/camel.html
Get a quick summary of camel facts.

Index